CLASSROOM DECOR

Decorate Your Classroom from Bulletin Boards to Time Lines

by Denise Bieniek, M.S.

Illustrated by Patrick Girouard

10 9 8 7 6 5 4 3 2

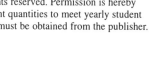

Troll CREATIVE TEACHER IDEAS

Troll Creative Teacher Ideas was designed to help today's dedicated, time-pressured teacher. Created by teachers for teachers, this innovative series provides a wealth of classroom ideas to help reinforce important concepts and stimulate your students' creative thinking skills.

Each book in the series focuses on a different curriculum theme to give you the flexibility to teach any given skill at any time of the year. The wide range of ideas and activities included in each book are certain to help you create an atmosphere where students are continually eager to learn new concepts and develop important skills.

We hope this comprehensive series will provide you with everything you need to foster a fun and challenging learning environment for your students. **Troll Creative Teacher Ideas** is a resource you'll turn to again and again!

Titles in this series:

Classroom Decor:
Decorate Your Classroom from Bulletin Boards to Time Lines

Creative Projects: Quick and Easy Art Projects

Earth Alert: Environmental Studies for Grades 4-6

Explore the World: Social Studies Projects and Activities

Healthy Bodies, Healthy Minds

Holidays Around the World: Multicultural Projects and Activities

It All Adds Up: Math Skill-Building Activities for Grades 4-6

Learning Through Literature:
Projects and Activities for Linking Literature and Writing

Story Writing: Creative Writing Projects and Activities

Think About It: Skill-Building Puzzles Across the Curriculum

The World Around Us: Geography Projects and Activities

World Explorers: Discover the Past

Metric Conversion Chart

1 inch = 2.54 cm	1 foot = .305 m	1 yard = .914 m
1 mile = 1.61 km	1 fluid ounce = 29.573 ml	1 cup = .24 l
1 pint = .473 l	1 teaspoon = 4.93 ml	1 tablespoon = 14.78 ml

Contents

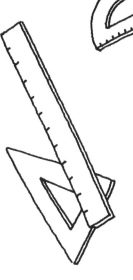

Center Labels 5-9

Dinosaur Days 10

Archaeological Dig 11

Behind-the-Scenes Mythology 12

Hieroglyphic Stories 13

Ancient Egyptian Museum 14

Infommercials 15

Time Capsules 16

Math Scramble Bulletin Board 17

North American Facts Bulletin Board 18

Bill of Rights Thoughts 19

The Book Shop 20

Culture Banners 21

Have You Heard This Nursery Rhyme? 22

Holiday Time Line 23

Taking Inventory 24

Multiplication Ice Cream 25-26

Skiing on Grammar Mountain 27-28

Reflective Winter Scene 29

Spring into Life 30

Spring Mosaics 31

Fall Forest Fractions 32-34

Fall Shadow Box 35

Ferris Wheel Message Board 36-37

Roman Numerals Activity Folder 38-39

A Whale of a Tale Bulletin Board 40-42

Traffic Jam Stories 43-44

Word Associations...45-46

Geometric Figures 47

Young Reviewers..48-49

Class Library 50

Student Storage 51

Metric Bodies 52

Hallway Pass...53

Holiday Gift Magnets 54-56

Expansion Time Line 57-60

Today's News 61-62

Decorative Borders..63-67

Dinosaur Posters 68-71

Division Dogs 72-74

Holiday Stencils 75-80

Homemade Paint 81

All That Glitters...82

Prehistoric Artists 83

Research Race Poster 84-86

The Seven Continents 87-92

Note to Parents 93

Awards...94-96

Center Labels

Create learning centers in the classroom that are well-stocked, labeled, and clearly identifiable. Try to build enthusiasm for the centers by talking about them with the class: ask what they think should be included in particular centers, what uses they could make of certain centers, and where the best area in the room might be for each center. Later, when the centers are ready to use, have a formal unveiling.

Stock a classroom library or reading center with books that are at, below, and above the students' reading levels. Try to display a variety of reading materials, such as drama, comic books, how-to books, joke and riddle books, comedies, mysteries, and other genres of literature. Make the area inviting by spreading out some pillows or by placing some old blankets on the floor. Put up some posters or students' work having to do with reading, such as reports students have written about books they have read, or a book review list. As each student completes a book, he or she may write a short review. These reviews may be made into a handbook and left in the library for others to read and use when selecting new reading material.

Stock a math center with manipulatives, such as base-ten blocks, counters, cuisenaire rods, geoboards, and calculators. Activities for students to try at the center should be easily accessible. You may wish to place posters illustrating various math concepts on the walls of the center.

A writing center must have certain items in it to be successful: different types and sizes of paper, various writing tools, a dictionary, a thesaurus, a grammar book, and a typewriter or computer (if possible). A time for writing should be set aside every day. Begin with short sessions and gradually add time to the sessions. Hold a short meeting with students to discuss the current writing topic(s), and then allow plenty of time for rough drafts, editing, and conferencing. Allow students to discuss their writing and offer help to others who seek it. Hold a sharing time at the end of the session to address comments or questions.

A current events area might be stocked with newspapers, magazines, and a radio. Students should be encouraged to bring in articles they find interesting or confusing. Time may be set aside each day or week for discussion of world, local, and national events. Arrange the students' articles and others you find thought-provoking on the wall of the center. To encourage students to read the articles, ask the class an open-ended question at the start of the day about some event discussed in an article posted on the wall. At the end of the day ask the question again and discuss it for a few minutes.

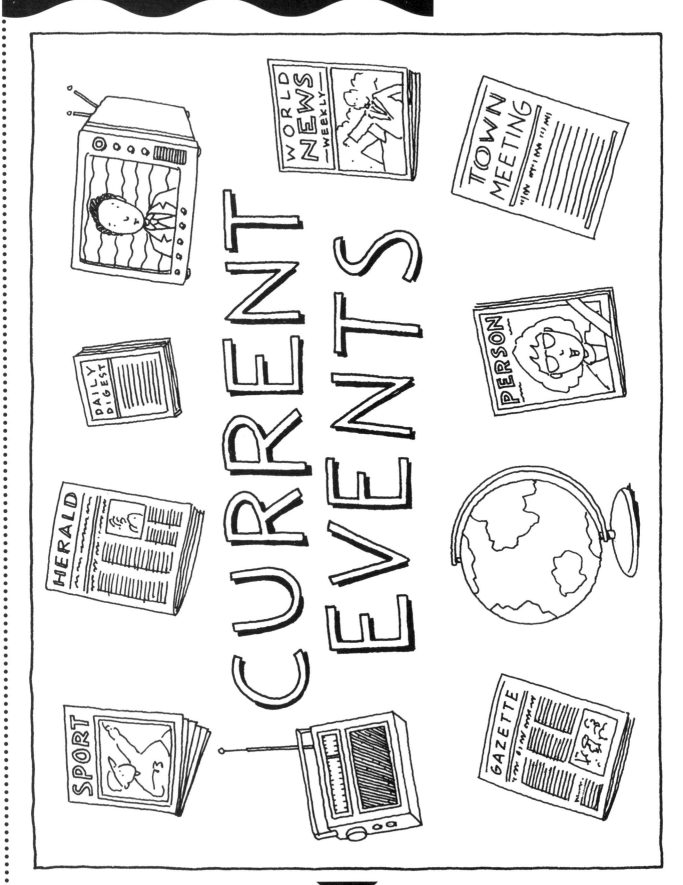

CURRENT EVENTS

Center Labels

Dinosaur Days

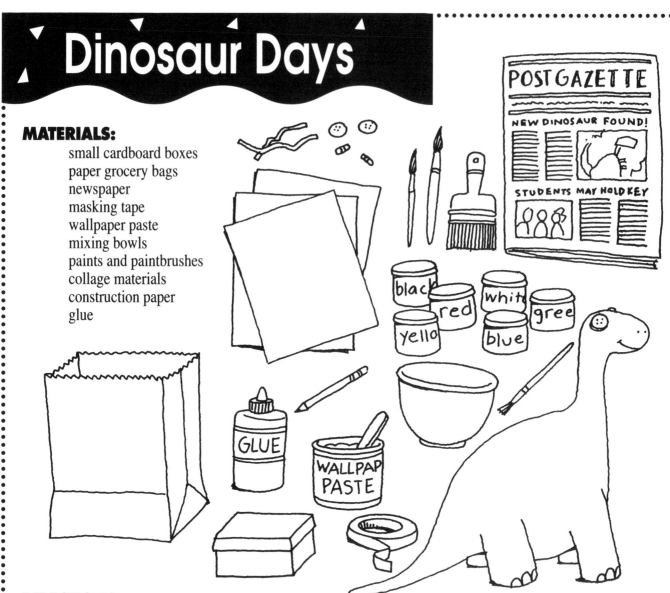

MATERIALS:

small cardboard boxes
paper grocery bags
newspaper
masking tape
wallpaper paste
mixing bowls
paints and paintbrushes
collage materials
construction paper
glue

DIRECTIONS:

1. Encourage students to borrow books from the library to research the different types of dinosaurs. Ask each student to choose one in which he or she is interested. Inform the class that they will be making minidinosaurs.

2. Distribute small cardboard boxes and paper grocery bags to students to use to form the basic shape of their chosen dinosaur. Show students how to tape the sections together with masking tape.

3. Have students use newspaper to fill in the grocery bags and give them shape. The newspaper may also be used to add features to the dinosaurs, such as horns, tails, or other shapes too difficult to sculpt using the boxes and bags.

4. In a mixing bowl, mix a cup of wallpaper paste with enough water to make the mixture thick, but pourable. Rip newspaper into strips. Show students how to dip the strips into the paste and wipe off the excess between two fingers.

5. Have students lay the strips over the entire surface of each dinosaur, making sure to smooth them. Cover each dinosaur with at least three layers of newspaper, placing each layer on with the print facing a different direction. Allow the dinosaurs to dry.

6. When the dinosaurs have dried, provide students with many colors of paint to use to decorate their dinosaurs. Students may paint their dinosaurs and then glue on any materials they wish to complete them, such as yarn for hair, construction paper for scales, or feathers for wings.

7. Ask each student to write a short essay on the dinosaur he or she has chosen to make. The essays should include the formal name of the dinosaur, where it lived, when it lived, what it ate, and what sort of protective devices it possessed to use against predators.

8. Display the dinosaurs in the science center along with students' essays.

Archaeological Dig

MATERIALS:

- plaster of Paris
- mixing bowls
- rubber gloves
- small plastic plates with rim
- oil

DIRECTIONS:

1. Follow the directions on the container of plaster of Paris. Wear rubber gloves to prevent the mixture from getting on your hands.

2. Pour the mixture into a plastic plate. Before it hardens, rub some oil on an everyday object, such as a key or a crayon, and press it lightly into the plaster. Remove it right away. Leave the plaster to harden. Repeat, using some objects with which the students will be familiar and some with which they will not.

3. Brainstorm with the class about the study of archaeology. Write all comments on the chalkboard. Then inform the class that they are going to pretend they are archaeologists and piece together clues to solve a mystery.

4. Pass the first plaster "fossil" around for students to feel and observe. When it has gone around once, ask the class to guess what it is and what its use might be. Proceed to the more unusual fossils.

5. When students are done looking at the fossils, have them come, two at a time, to a space set aside in the classroom for making more fossils. Students may choose something in the room or something from home with which to make their own. Try to keep the students separate as they create their fossils so no one will know what the others have made.

6. Once the fossils have been completed, ask the students to write their names on the backs and cover them.

7. Lay the fossils out around the tables and assign a number to each one. Ask students to walk around the room, observing and gently touching the fossils. Have them try to identify each one and write down their guesses on a piece of paper.

8. When all fossils have been seen, call out the assigned numbers and ask each child to identify his or her fossil.

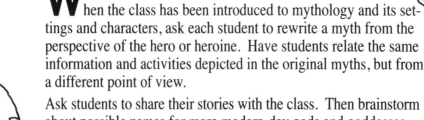

Behind-the-Scenes Mythology

When the class has been introduced to mythology and its settings and characters, ask each student to rewrite a myth from the perspective of the hero or heroine. Have students relate the same information and activities depicted in the original myths, but from a different point of view.

Ask students to share their stories with the class. Then brainstorm about possible names for more modern-day gods and goddesses. When all the names have been recorded, ask the class to explain the purpose of each one. If necessary, give the students an example to start them off, such as Environmentia, goddess of a clean Earth.

Share the following story about Environmentia with the class:

The goddess named Environmentia lives in a far-off place called Shipshape. Shipshape is so far above Earth that Environmentia can see everything that goes on in the world.

One day, she looked down and watched as a group of humans walking along a street threw their garbage onto the ground. Environmentia was very upset. She began to decay, because every time she recorded an action needlessly hurting Earth, she fell apart just a little. But every time she saw an act for the good of Earth, she would turn green.

Environmentia stood there decaying and decided to teach the humans a lesson. That night, while the humans slept, she programmed a dream into their minds. They dreamed that giants had come to live among them in their neighborhoods. The giants dropped their trash wherever they felt like. Soon everyone's homes were covered in garbage, their streets were so littered they could not walk out the doors, their food supplies ran low, and their water was contaminated! On and on the horrors progressed until the humans all awoke from their dreams screaming.

From that day on, those humans placed trash where it belonged. Environmentia sighed with relief and turned a bit more green.

But, inside, Environmentia was still angry. How could those people just drop their junk wherever they chose? Why couldn't these humans just hold onto their trash and wait until they found the proper receptacle? Earth was falling apart! And it wasn't easy keeping track of these humans. They were everywhere, throwing their garbage on beaches, in the water, in the forest. How many times did she have to warn them?

But before Environmentia got too angry, a little boy and girl started picking up the garbage in a park. Environmentia started turning greener and greener.

"Maybe there is hope for humans after all," she said.

Have the class offer different versions of Environmentia's story. Then ask them to create their own modern-day gods and goddesses, similar to Environmentia. Remind them to include the god's or goddess's name and reason for being, an episode about something the god or goddess did, and a last paragraph giving the reader the hero's or heroine's perspective.

Encourage each student to illustrate a scene from the myth or draw a picture of the mythical creature. Set up a mythology gallery and display the works in the art center.

Hieroglyphic Stories

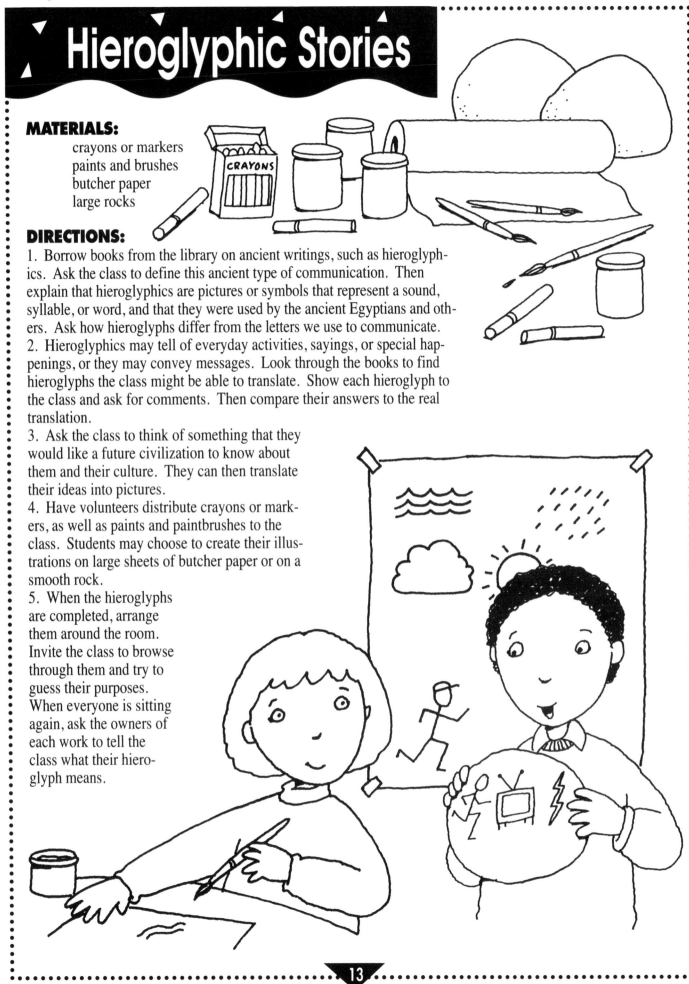

MATERIALS:

crayons or markers
paints and brushes
butcher paper
large rocks

DIRECTIONS:

1. Borrow books from the library on ancient writings, such as hieroglyphics. Ask the class to define this ancient type of communication. Then explain that hieroglyphics are pictures or symbols that represent a sound, syllable, or word, and that they were used by the ancient Egyptians and others. Ask how hieroglyphs differ from the letters we use to communicate.

2. Hieroglyphics may tell of everyday activities, sayings, or special happenings, or they may convey messages. Look through the books to find hieroglyphs the class might be able to translate. Show each hieroglyph to the class and ask for comments. Then compare their answers to the real translation.

3. Ask the class to think of something that they would like a future civilization to know about them and their culture. They can then translate their ideas into pictures.

4. Have volunteers distribute crayons or markers, as well as paints and paintbrushes to the class. Students may choose to create their illustrations on large sheets of butcher paper or on a smooth rock.

5. When the hieroglyphs are completed, arrange them around the room. Invite the class to browse through them and try to guess their purposes. When everyone is sitting again, ask the owners of each work to tell the class what their hieroglyph means.

13

Ancient Egyptian Museum

Borrow books on ancient Egypt from the library. Divide the class into groups to research different aspects of life in ancient Egypt. Students may want to research government, jobs, the role of women and men, schooling, or the climate.

When each group has finished researching, allow them to present their material to the rest of the class. Encourage students to comment on or ask questions about the presentations. After the presentations, inform the class that they will be making a museum of ancient Egypt based on the information they have gathered. Give the groups some time to come up with ideas for displays in their areas of research.

Ideas for their displays include: clothing, recreation, food, burial, furniture, homes, eating utensils, the pyramids, and the Sphinx. For example, students may make a sarcophagus from a shoe box. The exterior may be painted gold and then a face and body may be painted on the lid showing who is buried there. A doll may be "mummified" by wrapping it in gauze and placing it inside the box. Directions for mummifying can be attached to the bottom of the box.

Or students may wish to create a papier-mâché Sphinx. To form the shape of the Sphinx, wad up newspaper and tape it in place until the form is recognizable. Students can then cover their shapes with papier-mâché and paint them.

Arrange the displays around the room with appropriate backdrops if possible. Let each group be the tour guide for their own display. Invite other classes into the room to visit the museum. The tour guides may explain their displays and answer any questions the visitors may have. (Have those research books handy, just in case!)

Infommercials

MATERIALS:

crayons or markers
construction paper, cut to shoe-box width
transparent tape
shoe boxes
scissors
paper towel rolls

DIRECTIONS:

1. Ask the class to come up with the names of jobs in which they are interested. Encourage each child to choose one and explain why he or she would be interested in a career in that particular field.

2. Ask the class if anyone knows what an "infommercial" is. Explain that an "infommercial" is a commercial, usually about a half-hour long, designed to give information to the public. Some infommercials are about products, some talk about how to become a better person, some are for political causes, and some are about making money.

3. Inform the class that they will be making infommercials about jobs. They should choose job they like and then decide what the highlights are. Each student should feature aspects of the job that will make other people want to train or study for it.

4. Once each child has an outline of his or her ideas, have the child record each piece of information on a separate piece of paper. Tell students to make an introductory page for each job as well.

5. When all the pages are finished, they can be taped to one another, top to bottom: first the introductory page, then the second page taped to the bottom of the first, the third page taped to the bottom of the second, and so on, until all the pages have been taped together.

6. To make the televisions, discard the shoe box tops. Demonstrate to the class how to cut a rectangle away from the bottoms of their shoe boxes. Demonstrate how to cut pairs of holes in each side panel that are big enough for the paper towel rolls to fit through. The holes on each side should match up with those on the opposite side, as shown.

7. Stand the shoe boxes on one end with the bottom facing away. Show students how to insert one paper towel roll through the bottom holes. Then tape the bottom of the last page of the infommercial to the roll. Turn the paper towel roll until all the pages are wrapped around it, with the introductory page on top.

8. Insert another paper towel roll in the top holes. Tape the top of the first page onto the roll.

9. When the pages are in place, turn the "television" around. To run the infommercial, hold the top roll on each side and turn it away from the viewer. To rewind, hold the bottom roll on each side and turn it toward the viewer.

10. Set aside one area of the room for these "career infommercials." Encourage the class to view all of them. Decorate the area with pictures and books showing people performing the jobs described. If possible, have visitors come to the class to talk about their jobs and, if applicable, their uniforms.

Time Capsules

Create a time line with the class about human achievements from their primitive beginnings to their relative sophistication today. Display the time line along a wall or bulletin board.

Ask the class to think about which time period they would like to have lived in. When students respond, ask them to explain their choices. Then inform students that they will be making time capsules.

Explain that time capsules are containers holding objects from a certain time frame that are to be opened at a future date. These objects may be documents, recordings, household items, art, clothing, or anything reflecting the particular time or culture.

Encourage students to choose a time period and begin collecting objects from that era.

Inform the class that they will be trying to guess the time period of each other's capsules and ask each student not to share his or her choice with anyone. Objects need not be original; they may be replicas or items crafted to resemble the real things. For example, a student interested in making a time capsule from the early pioneering days might make a covered wagon using craft sticks, fabric, and jar lids.

When the capsules are completed, invite each student to present his or her objects to the class without revealing the chosen time frame. After each presentation, allow time for the class to ask questions and guess the time period. Presenters may reveal their time frames after all comments and questions.

Math Scramble Bulletin Board

LIFT FOR ANSWERS ↓

MATERIALS:

bulletin board paper
stapler
5" x 7" index cards
markers
yarn
sticky-backed Velcro

DIRECTIONS:

1. Cover a bulletin board with bright paper.
2. Decide which math terms are suitable for the level of the class and how many terms are to be covered. Some suggestions are: place value, ordinal numbers, negative numbers, Venn diagrams, prime numbers, Roman numerals, multiplication, division, improper fractions, common denominators, decimals, percentage, angles, trapezoid, area, and circumference. Write each term on a 5" x 7" index card, scrambling the letters in each word.
3. Staple these cards to the middle of the bulletin board. Cut as many lengths of yarn as there are cards, each about 25" long. Knot one end of each yarn length and staple that end to the top of each card.

4. On the remaining cards, write an example of each math term. Staple these cards around the edges, not too far from their matching math term card. On the top of the example cards, stick a small piece of Velcro, making sure it is from the hard half of the strips.
5. Students must unscramble the math terms and then find the matching example among the cards along the edges of the board. When they have found the match, they should pick up the free end of the yarn attached to the scrambled math term card and place it on the Velcro of the matching card.
6. To allow students to self-check, attach an answer sheet nearby. When they are finished, they can check their work on their own.

North American Facts Bulletin Board

I AM THE SMALLEST STATE WHICH AM I ?

MATERIALS:

bulletin board paper   stapler
5" x 7" index cards   markers

DIRECTIONS:

1. Cover a bulletin board with blue paper to suggest the oceans that surround North America. Staple a map of North America in the center of the bulletin board.

2. Fold 5" x 7" index cards in half. On the front flaps, write a question or riddle about an area that can be located on the map. Some examples are:

> I am the largest state. Which am I? (Alaska)
>
> Name the longest river in the United States. (Mississippi-Missouri)
>
> I am the tallest building in the United States. What am I called, and where am I located? (Sears Tower, Chicago, Illinois)
>
> What is the longest bridge span in North America called, and where is it located? (Verrazano-

> Narrows in New York City, New York)
>
> I am the state with the largest population. Which am I? (California)
>
> What North American country has the largest area? (Canada)

3. On the inside of each card, write the answer to the question. Staple the folded cards around the bulletin board.

4. To use the board, students may read the questions, find their answers on the map or in an encyclopedia or other reference book, and then check their answers by lifting the front cover of the cards. Change the questions every few days to challenge students with new facts.

Bill of Rights Thoughts

MATERIALS:

black bulletin board paper
stapler
white construction paper
tape
film projector
scissors
markers

DIRECTIONS:

1. Staple black paper to a bulletin board.
2. To make a profile picture of each student, ask a student to sit on a chair in front of a wall. Turn the chair sideways so that the student is sitting next to the wall.
3. Tape a piece of white construction paper on the wall behind the student. Next, place a film projector in front of the student and direct it toward the wall. Turn the projector on and shine the light on the student's head. Make sure the whole head is visible on the paper.
4. Using a pencil, trace the profile of the student. When the profile is finished, have the student cut it out.
5. After all the student profiles have been completed,

have a class discussion about the Bill of Rights. Ask the class to think about and share their interpretations of the Bill of Rights.
6. Have each child write a few sentences telling his or her thoughts about the Bill of Rights on the profile.
7. Staple a copy of the Bill of Rights to the center of the board and then add the profiles around it.
8. Encourage students to read their classmates' interpretations. Discuss any differences of opinion they may have. Remind the class that although they may not agree with someone, everyone is entitled to his or her opinion.

The Book Shop

Discuss with the class the contributions of women throughout history. Talk about the struggles of women to be heard and to take their places in politics, business, medicine, and other sectors of society.

Talk about women in various countries and their places in their societies. Compare and contrast the women the students know with women in societies in which women are not considered equal to men. What do they think their mothers, sisters, aunts, and other women they know would do if they were to find themselves in such an unequal society?

Inform the class that they will be reading biographies of women who have helped make contributions to the world. Students may choose a book of biography in any area in which they are interested— medicine, law, politics, human rights, the home, education, business, child care, construction, and so on.

When all the students have finished reading their chosen biography, have them pretend that they are in the advertising department of the publishing firm that published the book. Their job is to entice readers to buy the book they have read. Discuss the ways a book jacket might catch the attention of consumers. Mention that book publishers might use bright colors, an illustration from a climatic scene, a quotation from the book, or rave reviews about the content of a particular book.

Distribute construction paper, crayons or markers, scissors, glue, and collage materials to the class. Ask each student to make a book jacket for the book he or she has read. The jacket should include a front cover, a back cover, and inside flaps. Students may use the available materials to create a book jacket that they think will lure readers to read the book.

Display the jackets on a table or shelf. Behind them, create the feeling of a book shop by covering the wall with rows of books or a large illustration of a window with window shoppers looking in. Encourage students to decorate the area to make it look more like a book shop. They may add posters about books or reading, or make signs advertising a sale or a new book coming out. Have students browse through the book shop, examining each other's book jackets.

Discuss the techniques used by the students on their book jackets. Which were the most successful ones? Did any book jacket make them want to read the book? If possible, loan the display to the school library and see how many others students read the recommended books.

Culture Banners

MATERIALS:

felt
fabric scraps
different-colored threads and needles
fabric glue
collage materials

DIRECTIONS:

1. Ask volunteers to find out the cultural background of each student. Encourage students to borrow books from the library so they can research their own and their classmates' cultures.

2. Send home a student-made survey questioning parents and other relatives about their cultures. Some suggested areas to research are:

> food (what kinds, how it is prepared, how it is served, how it is eaten)
> holidays
> music
> family and relatives
> recreation

3. Talk about how students who have recently moved to this country might feel about the differences between their native cultures and the culture of their new home. Do students think most people would want to fit in as soon as possible, or would they feel more comfortable preserving their own familiar cultures? Do they think it is easier for young people or adults to adopt another culture? Do they think it is right to retain the culture of another country while living in a new one?

4. Have the class make banners to celebrate the different cultural backgrounds found in their region. The banners should reflect their own family histories as immigrants to this country or as Native Americans.

5. Display the banners along the classroom walls or hang them from the lights. Invite each student to explain his or her banner to the rest of the class.

Have You Heard This Nursery Rhyme?

Explain to the class that they will be creating their own nursery rhymes. Brainstorm on the titles of nursery rhymes they know. Then have each student choose one and, with a dictionary and thesaurus, begin rewriting it. For example, the rhyme "Mary Had A Little Lamb" can be retitled "Jamie Had A Great Big Pig" and the rhyme can be rewritten.

When each student has completed his or her rhyme, have a reading. Ask each child to read his or her rhyme, then have the class try to guess from which rhyme it came.

Ask students to illustrate their rhymes. Attach the rhymes and illustrations to a wall in a school hallway. People walking by can then enjoy the rhymes and try to figure out their origins. You may also wish to bind the rhymes and illustrations into a book and donate it to a lower grade.

Holiday Time Line

Create a year-long holiday time line with the class. Share with students the holidays you celebrate or feel are important in your own life. Then ask the class to talk about the holidays they celebrate at home. Enter the dates of these holidays on the time line as well. If the holidays change from year to year, mark the approximate time range in which they occur.

On a 4" x 6" index card, write down its name and date. Then have the students choose one or two holidays each to write on index cards, too. (Students should use different-colored markers to group the holidays by category (for example, red and blue for holidays celebrating events and people important in American history), or just to add color to the time line.) Keep making index cards until all the holidays on the time line have cards. If there is room, draw pictures illustrating the holiday.

On other 4" x 6" index cards, write down the reason a specific holiday is celebrated, any history connected with it, and any interesting stories about it. For example, Thanksgiving Day was first celebrated by the Pilgrims after they had survived their first year in America. We celebrate Thanksgiving each year on the fourth Thursday in November.

Punch a hole in the bottom left and bottom right corners of the first set of index cards. Then punch a hole in the top left and the right corners of the second set of index cards. Tie the cards together with brightly colored yarn.

Ask the class to sequence the two sets of cards and tie the sets together with brightly colored yarn, as shown. Hang them along a classroom wall or on a bulletin board. Make a banner with the title "Holiday Time Line" to place above it.

Taking Inventory

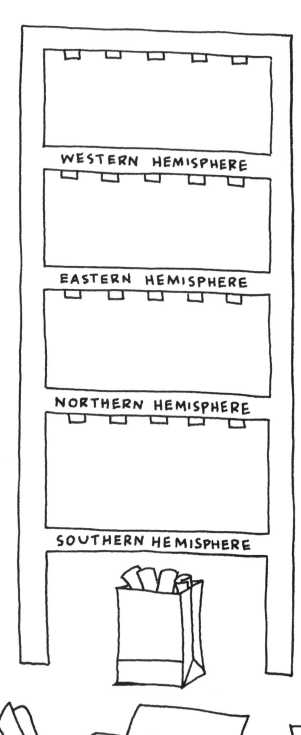

WESTERN HEMISPHERE

EASTERN HEMISPHERE

NORTHERN HEMISPHERE

SOUTHERN HEMISPHERE

WORLD ATLAS

MATERIALS:

brown construction paper
scissors
stapler
black marker
white construction paper
ribbon or yarn
Velcro
paper lunch bag or clear plastic bag

DIRECTIONS:

1. To make the "shelves" for this activity, cut strips about 2" wide and 2' long from brown construction paper. Arrange the strips on a wall or bulletin board and staple in place to resemble a cabinet having four shelves.

2. Along the base of each shelf, write one of the following labels: "Western Hemisphere," "Eastern Hemisphere," "Northern Hemisphere," and "Southern Hemisphere." On the top half of each shelf, attach five pieces of hard Velcro.

3. To make the maps that will be placed on the shelves, roll up twenty 6" x 6" pieces of white construction paper. Tie each one closed with a 6" length of ribbon or yarn. Distribute the maps so that there are five for each hemisphere.

4. On each rolled map, write the name of a country in a particular hemisphere. On the back of each one, attach a piece of soft Velcro. Add a paper lunch bag or a clear plastic bag to the base of the cabinet, and store all the maps inside.

5. To do the activity, ask a volunteer to pick a map from the bag and decide on which shelf it belongs. Some countries are in two hemispheres, so students will need to think about these countries' locations and choose the best place for each one.

6. To help students check their answers, place an atlas nearby.

24

Multiplication Ice Cream

MATERIALS:

crayons or markers bulletin board paper
scissors stapler
thumbtacks or pushpins

DIRECTIONS:

1. Reproduce the ice cream cone and ice cream scoop shapes on page 26 ten times each. Color the patterns and cut them out.
2. On each paper cone, write a number that can be divided evenly (for example, 48, which can be divided by 1 and 48, 2 and 24, 4 and 12, and 6 and 8.)
3. Divide the "scoops" among the "cones." On each paper scoop, write two numbers that, when multiplied, give the product written on the paper cone. For 48, for example, you may write *1 x 48* on one scoop, *4 x 12* on another, and so on.
4. Staple bulletin board paper to the board and add some features to remind students of summertime. Create a "counter" area and staple the paper cones in place on the counter. Ask some artistic students to draw a cash register and cashier and decorations for the store.
5. Place all the "scoops" in a "ice cream container" and staple it to the board. To make the container, wrap paper around a coffee can and decorate it to look like a particular ice cream flavor. Then tape a bottom to the paper. Slip the can out from the paper wrappings and staple the paper can to the bulletin board.
6. To use the activity, ask a volunteer to read the number on a particular cone and then find the ice cream scoops that match the product written on the cone. Have the students attach the scoops using thumbtacks or pushpins.
7. Change the numbers every few days to challenge the students.

Multiplication Ice Cream

Skiing on Grammar Mountain

MATERIALS:

crayons or markers
scissors
sticky-backed Velcro
blue bulletin board paper
white construction paper
stapler

DIRECTIONS:

1. Reproduce the skiers on page 28 ten times. Color the skiers and cut them out.

2. On each skier's skis, write a pair of homonyms, antonyms, or synonyms. Try to have an equal number of all three.

3. Attach a soft piece of Velcro to the back of each skier. Set aside.

4. Cover a bulletin board with blue paper. Using white construction paper, make three mountains, going from the base of the board to about 12" from the top. Make a signpost for each mountain. Call the first mountain "Homonym Hill," the second "Antonym Angle," and the third "Synonym Slope."

5. At random places on each mountain, attach six hard pieces of Velcro.

6. Ask a volunteer first to read the words on one of the skiers' skis and then decide whether the words are homonyms, antonyms, or synonyms. Once the child has determined what category the words belong to, he or she should attach the skier to the appropriate mountain.

7. To store the skiers, make a "ski shack" out of construction paper and staple it to a corner of the board around the sides and bottom. Leave the top open and slip the skiers into this opening. Make a sheet showing the answers to the activity and store it in the shack as well so that students may check their work.

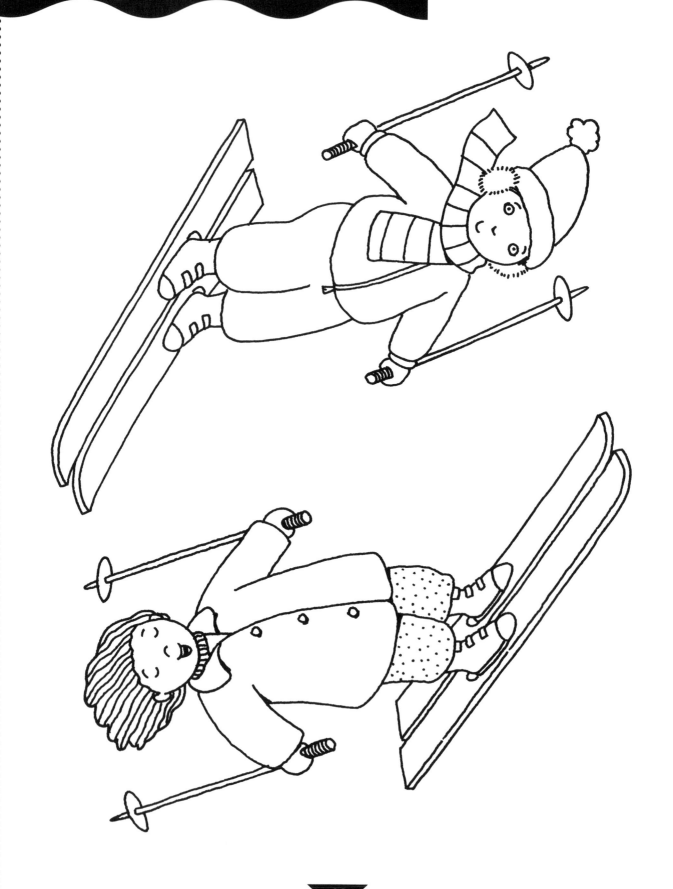

Reflective Winter Scene

Distribute a piece of white paper and a pencil to each student. Have students set up cups of black paint and thin brushes at each table. Ask them to think of a winter scene to paint that brings back good memories for them.

Encourage students to think for a few minutes before beginning their paintings. Have them keep their scenes fairly simple. They may then sketch their scenes in pencil. When they finish their sketches, have the students paint quickly over the pencil markings using the black paint and brushes.

Immediately after the painting is complete, have each student place a second piece of white paper over his or her work and gently press down until all areas of the painting have been smoothed out. Students should then remove the second paper and leave both to dry on a flat surface.

To put the display together, hang students' original paintings on a wall or bulletin board with the copies attached upside down, as shown. The bottom of the original should overlap slightly with the bottom of the copy. When the paintings are looked at, it will seem that the action is being reflected back, as though it were taking place by water. Entitle the bulletin board "Winter Reflections."

TAPE
EDGES →

Spring into Life

Explain to the class that many animals are born with particular features that enable them to survive in their habitats. Ask the class to give some examples of animals with special physical or behavioral characteristics that help them cope with the habitats in which they are born. (For example, the turtle is born with a protective shell, and dogs (and many other animals) have a keen sense of smell.)

Remind students that plants, too, have special features to survive in their habitats. One example is the cactus. Since the cactus does not need much water to grow and can take advantage of a short burst of rain, it is able to survive in the dry desert climate.

Divide the class into five groups. Have each group choose a habitat to design. Some suggestions are: desert, jungle, ocean, forest, and city.

Distribute large sheets of butcher paper, construc-tion paper, markers, glue, and collage materials to each group. Advise students to sketch their habitats before using the markers to color them in.

When the habitat pictures are finished, tape them to a wall, one next to one another. Then hand out 3" x 5" index cards to each student. Ask each child to write down the names of some animals and plants that can be found in his or her habitat.

Shuffle the cards and give one to each student. Gather the class together in a semicircle around the habitats. Call three students at a time to come up to the pictures and tape their cards below the appropriate habitats.

Have the rest of the class check each set of answers. Continue until all the cards have been used. Store the cards in a bag near the posters for students to use during free time.

Spring Mosaics

MATERIALS:

> different-colored crayon pieces
> grater, vegetable peeler, or pencil sharpener
> cups
> waxed paper
> scissors
> newspaper
> iron
> construction paper

DIRECTIONS:

1. Show the class how to shave crayons, demonstrating how to position fingers well away from the sharp edges of a grater, vegetable peeler, or pencil sharpener. Collect a cup of each color crayon. (Repeat this step if the shavings run out before the activity is completed.)

2. Inform the class that they will be making melted-crayon pictures. The first thing each student must do is sketch a drawing onto a piece of scrap paper.

3. To transfer the drawing onto waxed paper, lay a 9" x 12" piece of waxed paper down on a smooth, flat surface. Ask each student to choose the colors needed for his or her picture, and then drop small amounts of the chosen shavings onto the paper so it resembles the sketch.

4. When the shavings are all in place, heat up an iron. While it is heating, each student may lay another piece of waxed paper over the first, being careful not to move any shavings.

5. When the iron is hot, lay two sheets of newspaper over the waxed paper. Gently move the iron over the newspaper, smoothing over all parts of the picture. The crayon shavings will melt and cause the two pieces of waxed paper to stick together.

6. When the pictures have cooled, ask each student to cut a frame from construction paper. Hang the pictures on classroom windows so sunlight shining through will show the colors in them.

Fall Forest Fractions

MATERIALS:

crayons or markers   scissors   3" x 5" index cards
green bulletin board paper   stapler

DIRECTIONS:

1. Reproduce the art on pages 33 and 34 ten times. Have volunteers color the figures and cut them out.
2. Cover a bulletin board with green paper. Staple the trees all over the board in a random way so they resemble a forest. Staple a different number of leaves on each tree. At the foot of each tree, staple a different number of leaves again.
3. Staple a forest animal next to each tree. Leave an opening at the top of each animal. On it, write a question about the fraction of leaves on the ground or still on each tree. Some suggestions are:

What fraction of the tree's leaves are laying on the ground?
What fraction of the tree's leaves is still on the tree?
Which other tree has the same fraction of its leaves on the ground?
Which other tree has the same fraction of its leaves on the tree, but in its simplest form?
What is the fraction of the tree's leaves on the ground in its simplest form?
Add the fraction of the tree's leaves still on this tree and the fraction still on the tree next to this one.
Subtract the fraction of the tree's leaves on the ground with the fraction of the tree below this one's leaves on the ground.

4. Cut 3" x 5" index cards into 1" x 5" strips. Write the answers to the questions on these strips. To use the activity, students will read the question next to each tree, answer the question, then find the answer card and insert it behind the animal next to the tree.
5. Write the answers on a piece of paper and store the answer key near the bulletin board so students can check their answers. To store the answer cards, staple a forest animal to the bottom right corner of the bulletin board, making sure to leave the top open, and place the answer cards behind it.

Fall Forest Fractions

Fall Forest Fractions

Fall Shadow Box

MATERIALS:

shirt boxes
paints and paintbrushes
glue
collected small fall and holiday items
scissors
old magazines

DIRECTIONS:

1. Brainstorm with the class about items that remind them of the fall season. Things they may name may include pumpkins, Halloween costumes, turkeys, Pilgrims, changing leaf colors, colder weather, and return to school.

2. Ask each child to bring in a shirt box from home. Inform students that they will be making shadow boxes, small, shallow boxes hung on a wall and used for displaying small items.

3. Once everyone has a box, have each student paint the interior any fall color he or she chooses.

4. Have each student glue small items that reflect the season or the holidays occurring in the fall (such as acorns or leaves) inside the box. Students may also wish to cut out pictures from old magazines to use to decorate their shadow boxes.

5. Hang the shadow boxes around the classroom and allow time for the class to view and comment.

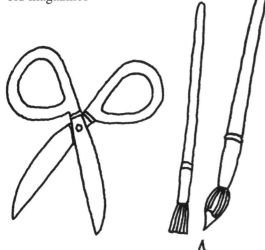

Ferris Wheel Message Board

MATERIALS:

crayons or markers   scissors
clear contact paper   permanent black marker
black construction paper   glue
blue bulletin board paper   tape

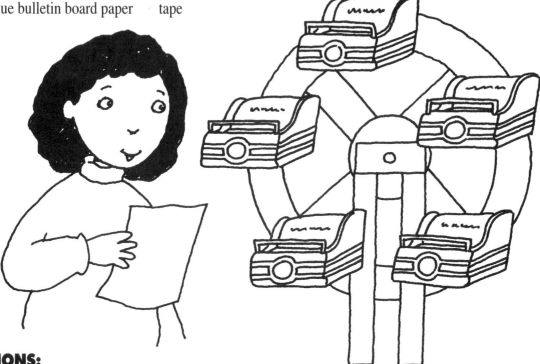

DIRECTIONS:

1. Reproduce the art on page 37 as many times as desired. Have volunteers color the Ferris wheel cars and cut them out.

2. On each car write a category name identifying what kind of message can be found inside. For example, one car may contain a record of the week's homework assignments. Students who have been absent can go to the Ferris wheel, find the car marked *Homework* and write down the assignments they missed. Another car may be used for field trip information and extra permission slips. A list of trips for that week or month may be posted in this car, as well as a list of materials students might need for the trips.

3. Have volunteers trace each car shape on construction paper, cut out the shapes, and glue the construction paper and car shapes together around the sides and bottom. Be sure the tops are left open.

4. Cover the cars with clear contact paper.

5. To make the Ferris wheel structure, cut a large circle from the black construction paper. Then cut out the center, leaving a 2"-wide strip around the

circumference.

6. Cut a smaller circle about 5" in diameter, from the construction paper. Lay the two circles on a table, placing the smaller circle inside the larger one.

7. Cut 2"-wide strips of black construction paper to connect the larger circle with the inner circle. Glue these strips from the small circle to the large circle, as shown.

8. Cut two more strips, also 2" wide, to be the legs of the wheel. Glue these to the small circle and extend them out past the large circle so they reach about 6" beyond the Ferris wheel.

9. Tape blue paper to a bulletin board. Make sure it is at eye level for students of average height. Then tape the Ferris wheel structure to the blue paper. Arrange the cars around the large wheel and glue them in place.

10. If desired, place a title above the Ferris wheel, such as "Class Reminders." Call students' attention to the Ferris wheel each morning to remind them of things they may have forgotten or missed.

Ferris Wheel Message Board

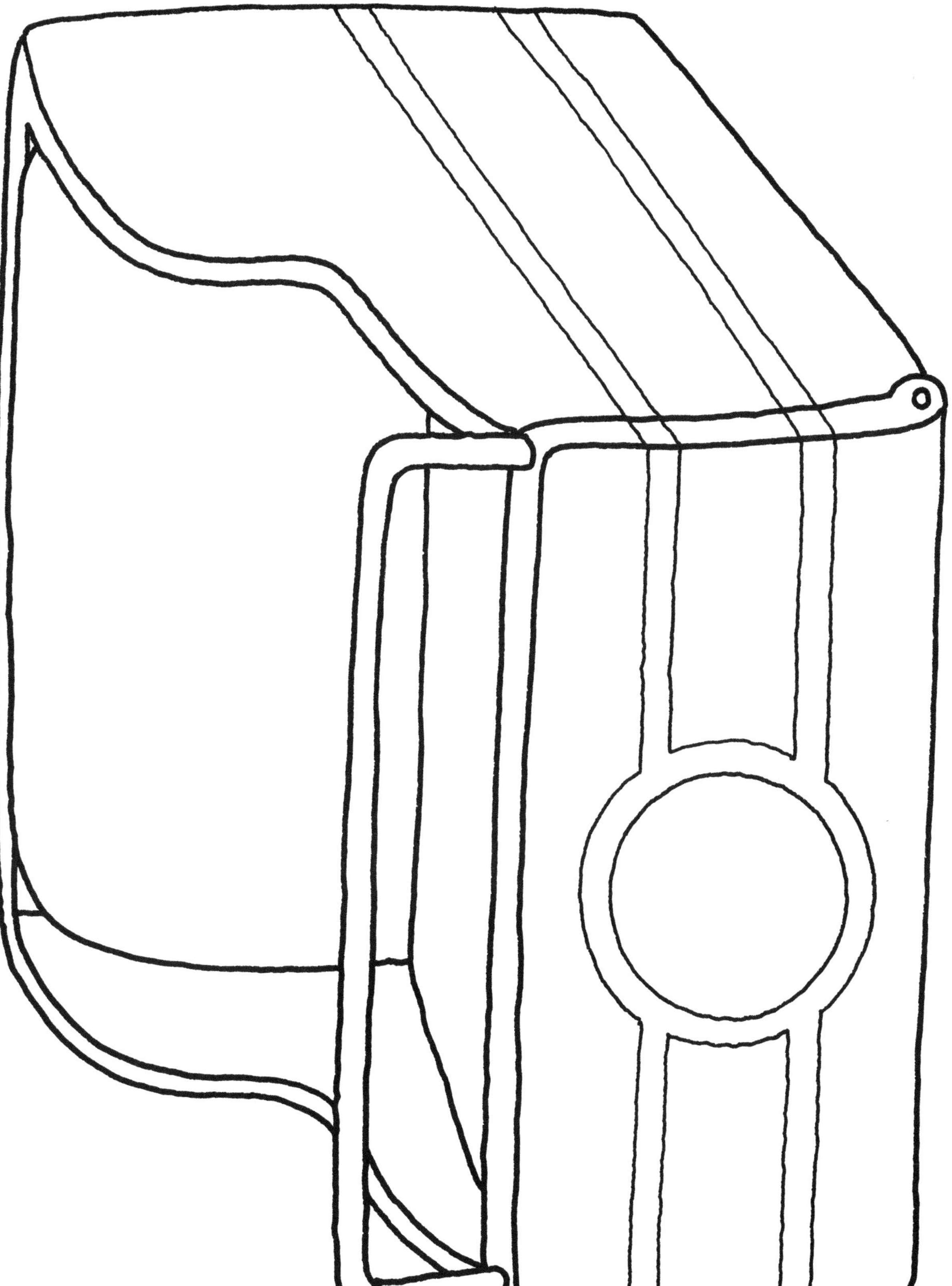

Roman Numerals Activity Folder

MATERIALS:

crayons or markers
scissors
oaktag
glue
clear contact paper
sticky-backed Velcro
folder with pockets inside

DIRECTIONS:

1. Reproduce the scribe and the tablets on page 39 ten times. Have volunteers color the scribes (but not the tablets).

2. Mount all the patterns on oaktag and cut them out. Cover with clear contact paper.

3. On each scribe's chest, write a number. On each tablet, write the same number in Roman numerals.

4. Attach a hard piece of Velcro to both of each scribe's hands. Attach a soft piece of Velcro to the back of each tablet.

5. Have students match the numbers on the scribes with the Roman numerals on the tablets. Ask them to place the appropriate tablet on each of the scribe's hands. To allow them to check their work, write the answers on the back of a pocket folder.

6. Store the scribes and the tablets in the pockets of the folder. Place the folder in the math center for students to use during free time.

Roman Numerals Activity Folder

A Whale of a Tale Bulletin Board

Borrow some books of tall tales from the school library. Explain to the class that a tall tale is an exaggerated story: a tall tale may begin as a telling of a real event, but after being told and embellished with each retelling, the tale turns into one of legendary proportions.

After the class has read one or more of the tall tales, reproduce the whale art on pages 41 and 42 once for each student. Have students color their whales, cut them out, and tape the two parts of the body together. Ask students to write their own tall tales inspired by the tall tales they have read or had read to them. Suggest that they write about something that has occurred in class, in history, or to someone they know, whether at home or on vacation. The tale should

begin as a real story but become exaggerated as it goes on.

Gather the students together for a reading of the tales. After each one, ask the class if the story was believable, and, if not, at what point they felt it became unbelievable. Students may offer constructive criticism at this point. After the readings, allow students to revise their tales if they like. When students are satisfied with their work, have them glue it into the centers of their whales.

Display the whales on a wall or a bulletin board under the title "A Whale of a Tale." Students who wish to create more stories should be encouraged to do so. Display these stories as well, or bind them into a class book and place them on a shelf in the reading center.

A Whale of a Tale Bulletin Board

A Whale of a Tale Bulletin Board

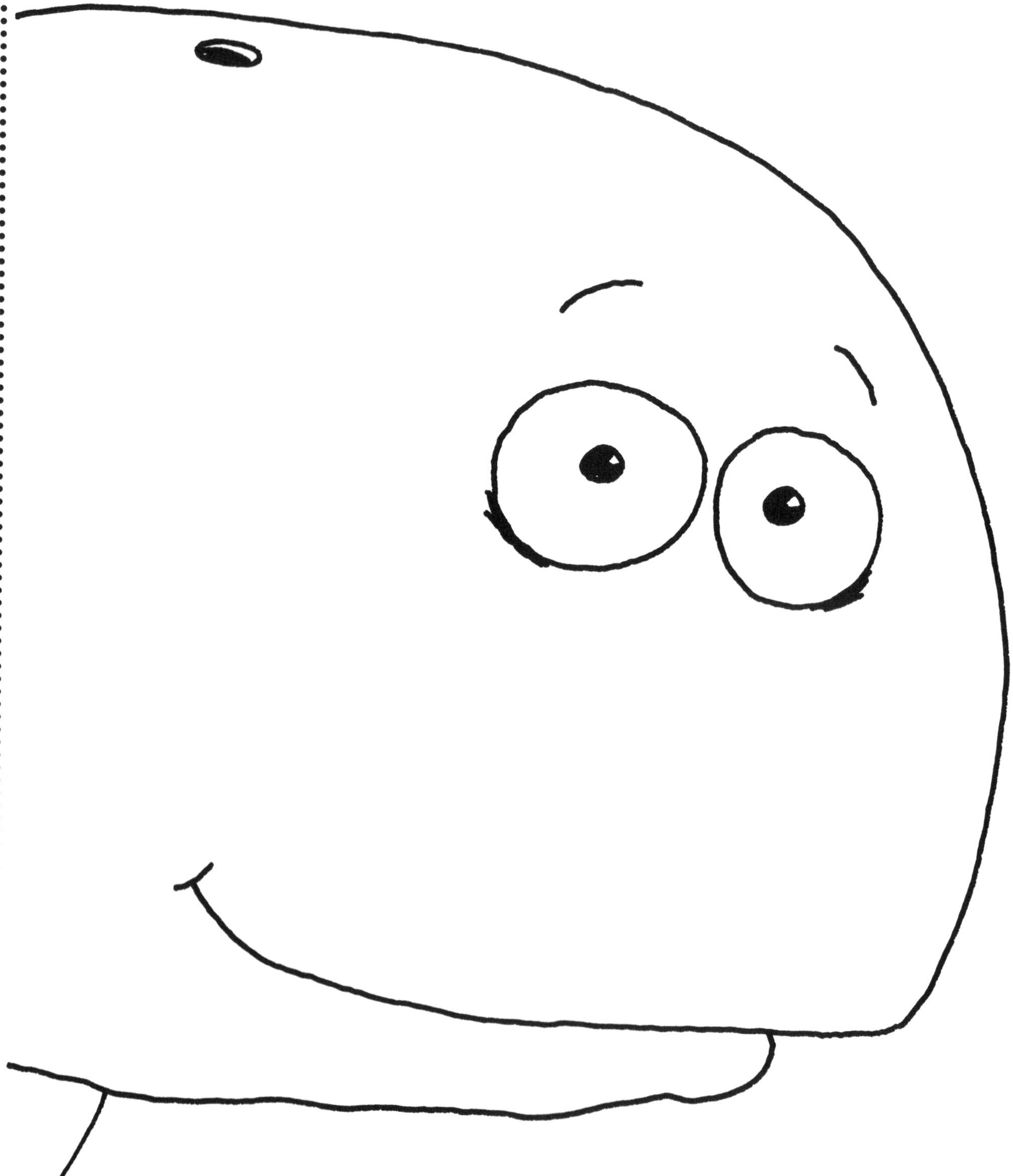

Traffic Jam Stories

Ask the students how many of them have ever been stuck in a traffic jam. Encourage them to talk about how they felt at the time and (apart from being able to move) what would have made the waiting better.

Mention that sometimes a story makes the time pass more quickly. Inform the students that they will be making up a story together to entertain some children who are stuck in a traffic jam on the highway. Each child may add to the story as it goes along.

To create the traffic jam, cover a board or wall space with blue paper. Cut black construction paper to form a road running over the bottom half of the paper. Add detail to the scene, such as sun, clouds, buildings, trees, or deer and other animals.

Reproduce the truck pattern on page 44 once for each student. Have students cut out the trucks.

Ask a student volunteer to begin the story with two or three sentences. He or she should write the beginning of the story on a truck. Staple or tape the first truck to one end of the highway. Then ask another volunteer to continue the story, writing his or her part on another truck. As students add to the story, the traffic jam will become longer and longer.

Remind the last few students that they need to bring the story to a conclusion. When the last truck has been added, read the whole story to the class. Ask them if they are satisfied with the ending. If not, ask students to think of different endings and share them with the class. Place a title above the traffic jam story, such as "A Story to Pass the Time."

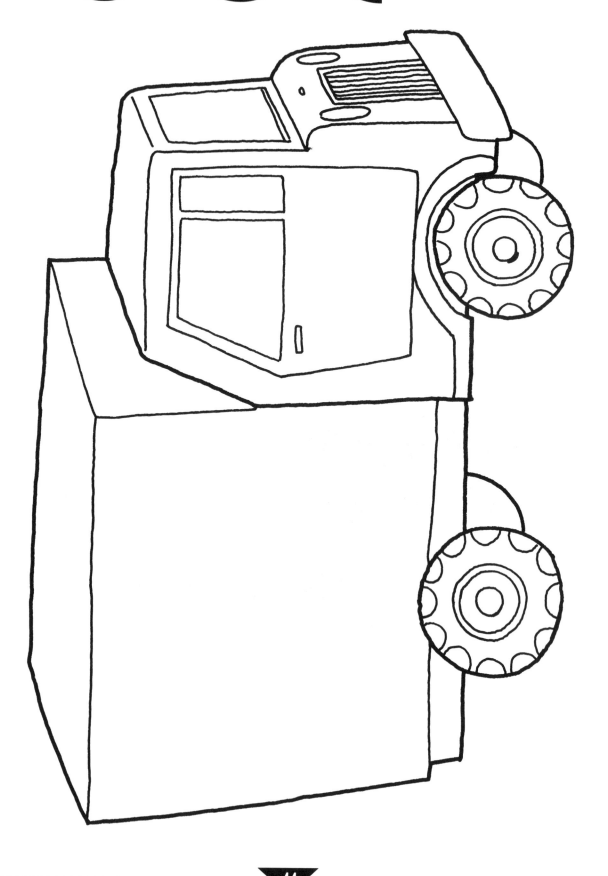

Word Associations

Ask the class what they think of when you say "socks and . . ." Most students will probably say "shoes." Explain that we often think of objects as paired with something else.

Ask students for a few examples of words they associate with others. Some suggestions are:

peanut butter and jelly   hat and coat
bride and groom   pencil and paper
spaghetti and meatballs   boys and girls
knife and fork   mother and father
bread and butter   hammer and nail

To do an activity based on this word association, reproduce the art on page 46 twenty times and ask volunteers to cut the shapes out. On one shape of each pair, write one of two words that go together, such as "socks" and "shoes." Write the second word of the pair on the other shape. Lightly tape the shapes to the chalkboard in random order.

Call a student to the board to pick out two words that go together and place them next to each other. Ask the student to explain the choice. He or she may then pick the next student to choose another pair. Continue until all the words have been paired.

Create new pairs and place them in a folder with pockets for students to use during free time.

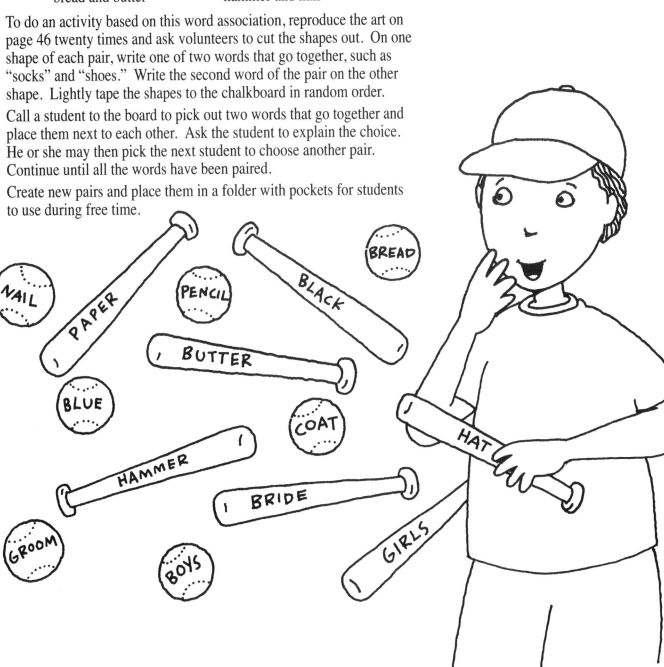

Word Associations

Geometric Figures

MATERIALS:
- pipe cleaners
- scissors
- colored cellophane
- glue
- styrofoam meat trays

DIRECTIONS:

1. Distribute pipe cleaners to the class. Ask students to twist the pipe cleaners into various geometric shapes: square, circle, rectangle, triangle, trapezoid, and parallelogram. Cut off any excess wire and twist the ends together so they will not open.

2. Have students twist the end of another pipe cleaner around the lower edge of the shapes to make a stand. (Do not make the stands too long, or they will not be able to support the weight of the shapes.)

3. Have students squeeze a line of glue around the shapes' outlines. Then cut pieces of colored cellophane slightly larger than each shape. Lay the shapes on the cellophane pieces and let dry. Trim off the excess.

4. Give a styrofoam meat tray to each student and demonstrate how to poke the end of the shape stands gently into it. Arrange the shapes so they do not touch. Make the stands different heights. If a stand cannot hold its shape upright, twist another pipe cleaner around it for extra support.

5. Display the geometric figures in the sunlight so the colors will be reflected on the furniture, wall, and floor.

Young Reviewers

DIRECTIONS:

1. Reproduce the book review sheet on page 49 several times for each student. Distribute the sheets to the class.

2. Ask if anyone knows what a book review is. Explain that newspapers, magazines, and television and radio shows often have a literary critic who reviews new books. The critic may praise a book or criticize it, but the review should explain why the critic thought the book was good or bad. People read or listen to the review to find out if they would be interested in buying the book. Critics can often influence how popular a book is.

3. Have each student write a review of a book he or she has recently read. Remind students that reviews may describe the plot of a book but shouldn't give away any surprises, twists, or the ending. Tell the class that their reviews should focus on whether or not they recommend the reviewed books and tell why or why not.

4. Post the reviews on a bulletin board or on a wall in the classroom reading center for all to see. Encourage students to continue reviewing more books for their classmates.

Young Reviewers

REVIEWED BY

TITLE

AUTHOR

REVIEW

Class Library

Reproduce the form below for students to fill out when borrowing a book from the class library. Be sure each book is clearly marked with the name of the teacher and the classroom number on the inside front cover. Choose one student to be the class librarian each week. The librarian should make sure the forms are filled out properly whenever books are borrowed and should file the forms inside a pocket folder. You may also wish to have the librarian follow up on any books that have been out on loan for longer than a set period of time.

TITLE:_____

AUTHOR:_____

DATE BORROWED:_____

BORROWER:_____

Student Storage

MATERIALS:

shoe boxes
crayons or markers
paints and paintbrushes
ribbon, yarn, buttons, tissue paper

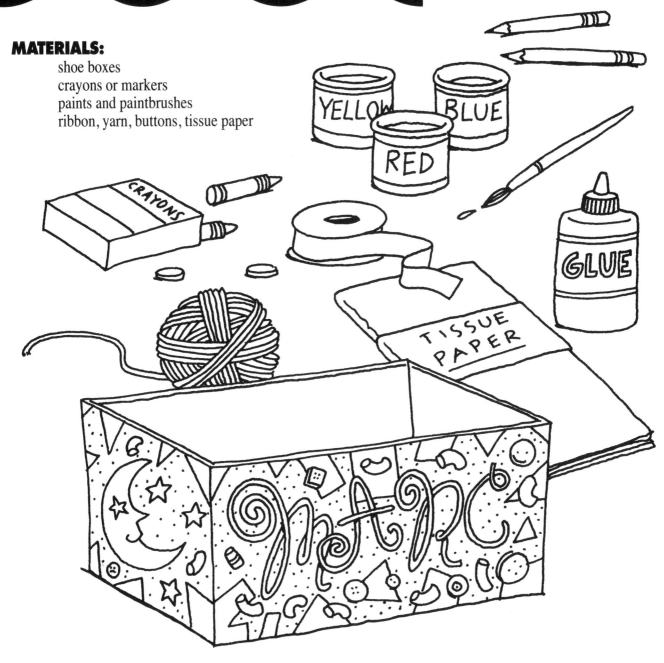

DIRECTIONS:

1. Ask each student to bring in from home the bottom of a small shoe box. Tell students that they will be using the shoe box to store pens, pencils, and other materials in their desks or cubbies.

2. Have each child write his or her name on the storage box. Students may write their names as fancifully as they wish.

3. Provide the class with paints and paintbrushes and with decorating materials such as ribbon, yarn, buttons, and tissue paper. Students may use these materials to personalize their storage boxes.

4. You may also wish to make storage boxes for other areas of the classroom. Ask volunteers to decorate shoe boxes or boot boxes according to the areas in which they will be used. For example, if a shoe box is used to store geoboards in the math center, a student may choose to decorate the box with math equations, math symbols, and other appropriate shapes.

51

Metric Bodies

Distribute long sheets of butcher paper to students. Have students pair up and trace each other's body outline on the paper. Ask students to cut their body outlines out and to color them.

Provide the class with several metric tape measures. Working in pairs, have each student write down some or all of the following measurements on his or her figure:

head	ankle
wrist	length of foot
arm	length of arm
waist	length of leg
leg	height

Next, give the class several standard tape measures. Have them write down these measurements next to the metric equivalents on the figures.

Using the chart on the right, show the different ways to convert metric measurements to the imperial measurements. Attach the figures to a bulletin board or to a wall in the math center under the title "Our Metric Bodies."

Measurement Conversions				
millimeters	x	.04	=	inches
centimeters	x	.39	=	inches
meters	x	3.28	=	feet
meters	x	1.09	=	yards
kilometers	x	.62	=	miles
inches	x	25.40	=	millimeters
inches	x	2.54	=	centimeters
feet	x	30.48	=	centimeters
yards	x	.91	=	meters
miles	x	1.61	=	kilometers

Hallway Pass

DIRECTIONS:

1. Reproduce the hallway pass on this page 20 times. Cut out the passes.

2. When a student needs to leave the classroom for another location in the building, fill out the pass.

3. The pass may also be used to send messages to other school workers. Write a message on the front of the pass. A return message may be written on the back of the pass.

NAME _____

ROOM _____

TO _____

DATE _____

TIME _____

SIGNED _____

Holiday Gift Magnets

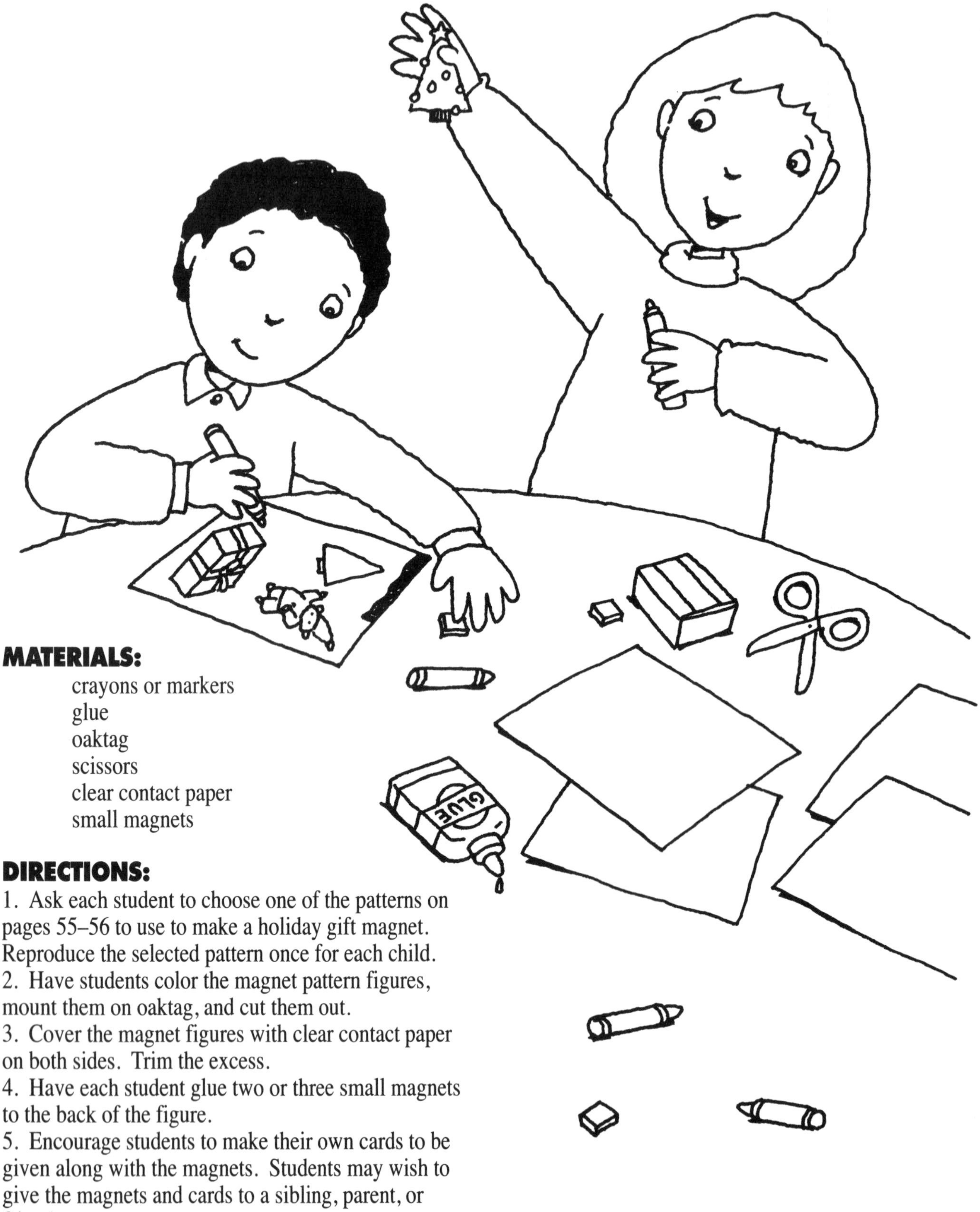

MATERIALS:

crayons or markers
glue
oaktag
scissors
clear contact paper
small magnets

DIRECTIONS:

1. Ask each student to choose one of the patterns on pages 55–56 to use to make a holiday gift magnet. Reproduce the selected pattern once for each child.

2. Have students color the magnet pattern figures, mount them on oaktag, and cut them out.

3. Cover the magnet figures with clear contact paper on both sides. Trim the excess.

4. Have each student glue two or three small magnets to the back of the figure.

5. Encourage students to make their own cards to be given along with the magnets. Students may wish to give the magnets and cards to a sibling, parent, or friend.

54

Holiday Gift Magnets

Holiday Gift Magnets

Expansion Time Line

1400   1492
Columbus sailed
from Spain and
arrives in the
West Indies.

1497   1500
John Cabot
arrives in
North America
from England.

DIRECTIONS:

1. Reproduce the patterns on pages 58–60 eight times. Have volunteers color the pattern figures and cut them out.

2. Tell the class that they will be working together to create a time line about the European exploration and settlement of North America. Begin by writing down students' suggestions about what should be included in the time line. Possibilities include:

1492	Columbus sails from Spain and arrives in the West Indies
1497	John Cabot arrives in North America from England
1513	Ponce de León explores Florida
1534	Jacques Cartier explores the Gulf of St. Lawrence in Canada
1607	Jamestown is settled by approximately 100 British colonists
1620	The Pilgrims settle in Plymouth Colony
1756	New York and Philadelphia are linked by stagecoach
1783	The Addition of 1783 extends the colonies to the Mississippi
1803	The Louisiana Purchase territory is acquired from France
1811	A national road joining the East and Midwest is begun
1825	The Erie Canal is opened, linking the Atlantic Ocean and the Great Lakes
1848	The California Gold Rush begins
1867	Alaska is bought from Russia
1903	The Wright Brothers make the first successful powered airplane flight
1959	Alaska and Hawaii become states

3. Use mural paper to make the time line. After drawing a thick, solid line down the length of the time line, mark off the years in periods of decades. Then have students fill in the dates and events that they have mentioned.

4. Attach one of the patterns to mark each historical event on the time line. Tell students to choose the figure representing the kind of transportation that most contributed to the exploration and expansion noted.

Expansion Time Line

Expansion Time Line

Expansion Time Line

Today's News

DIRECTIONS:

1. Reproduce the border pattern on page 62 many times. Ask volunteers to help color and cut out the border pieces.

2. Use the border pieces to frame an area of a bulletin board to be used for current events. Write the title "Today's News" at the top of the space inside the border.

3. Give the class a list of topics each week. Ask each child to bring in an article from a newspaper or magazine about one of the topics. Topics might include: elections, the military, science and technology, health, entertainment, education, the economy, and foreign affairs.

4. Have each student mount his or her article on construction paper and write a brief, one-paragraph summary of the current event. Ask the children to share their findings with the rest of the class. Encourage students to bring in articles that seem confusing or puzzling, and have students work together as a class to figure out what the issues are.

5. Mount the articles and summaries on the bulletin board under the "Today's News" heading.

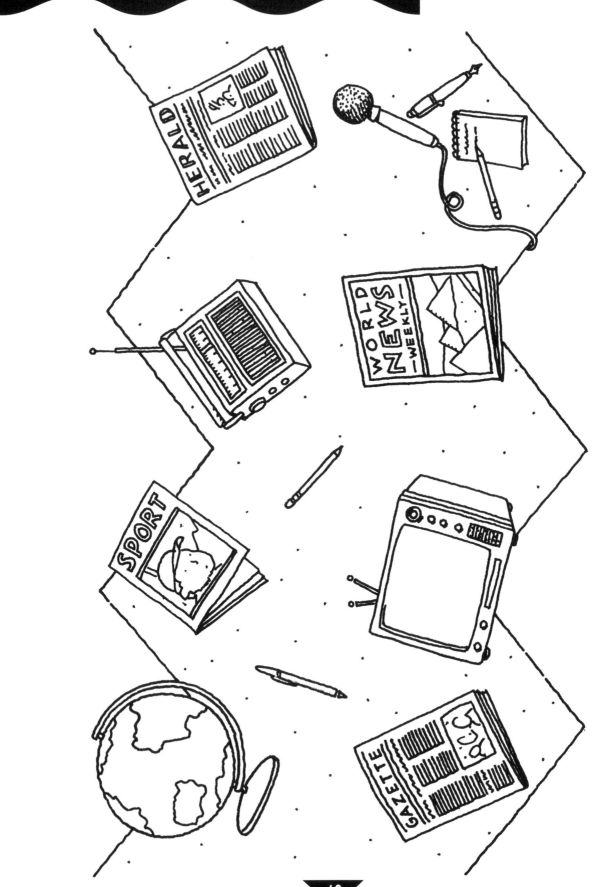

Decorative Borders

Use the border patterns on this page and pages 64–67 when working on study units with the appropriate themes. Reproduce each border as many times as necessary to frame an area of a bulletin board, classroom wall, or classroom perimeter. Ask volunteers to help color and cut out the border.

Decorative Borders

Decorative Borders

Decorative Borders

Decorative Borders

Dinosaur Posters

MATERIALS:

> crayons or markers
> scissors
> glue
> large piece of oaktag
> tape

DIRECTIONS:

1. Reproduce the dinosaur patterns on pages 69–71 once for each student. Have students color the patterns and cut them out.

2. Ask the children to do some research about dinosaurs. Allow students to borrow books from the school library and to use encyclopedias and other reference books to complete their research.

3. On a blank piece of paper, have each student write one or two sentences about each of the kinds of dinosaurs illustrated. Encourage students to trade papers with classmates to fact-check each other's work.

4. Give each student a large piece of oaktag. Have students arrange the dinosaurs on the oaktag however they wish, leaving enough room next to each figure to write about the kind of dinosaur shown.

5. Tell students to glue the dinosaurs in place and then copy the sentences they have written to describe each dinosaur. Hang the posters in the science center or along a school hallway for all to see.

DINO GLUE

68

Dinosaur Posters

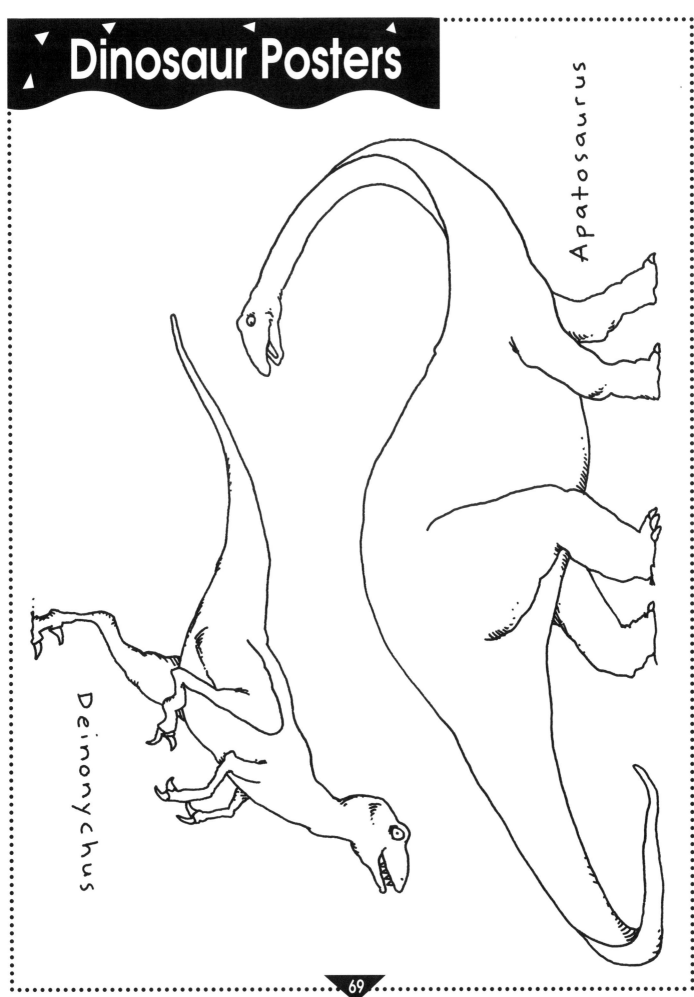

Apatosaurus

Deinonychus

Ankylosaurus

Stegosaurus

Dinosaur Posters

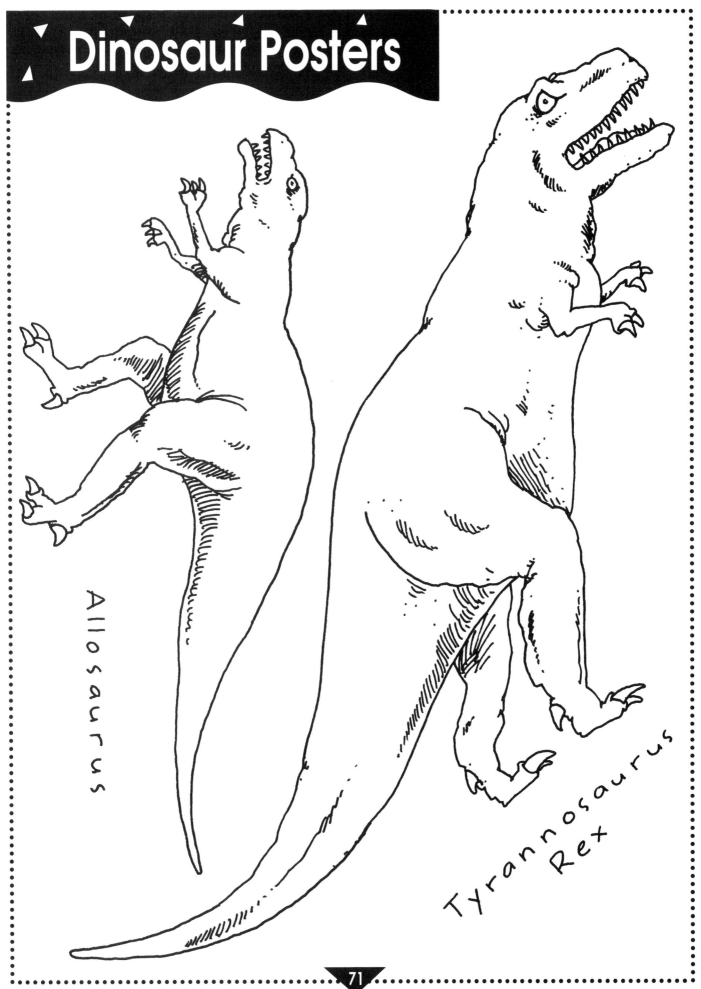

Allosaurus

Tyrannosaurus Rex

Division Dogs

DIRECTIONS:

1. Reproduce the dog patterns on pages 73–74 twelve times. Have volunteers color the patterns and cut them out.

2. Following the instructions in steps 3–6, use the dogs to form the parts of the division tables from 1 to 12. For example, if the numeral being studied is 6, the division sequence would be:

$$6 \div 1 = 6$$
$$12 \div 2 = 6$$
$$18 \div 3 = 6$$
$$24 \div 4 = 6$$
$$30 \div 5 = 6$$
$$36 \div 6 = 6$$
$$42 \div 7 = 6$$
$$48 \div 8 = 6$$
$$54 \div 9 = 6$$
$$60 \div 10 = 6$$
$$66 \div 11 = 6$$
$$72 \div 12 = 6$$

3. Write the numbers that are being divided and the number 6 on index cards. Place the numbers on the large dogs. Place the number 6 on the medium dogs.

4. Write the series of numbers from 1 to 12 on the small dogs.

5. Write the division signs and equals signs on index cards.

6. Attach the dogs in columns on a bulletin board to make the division table. Leave the division dogs up for as long as the class is studying the particular table involved. Then switch the index cards to make a new division table.

Division Dogs

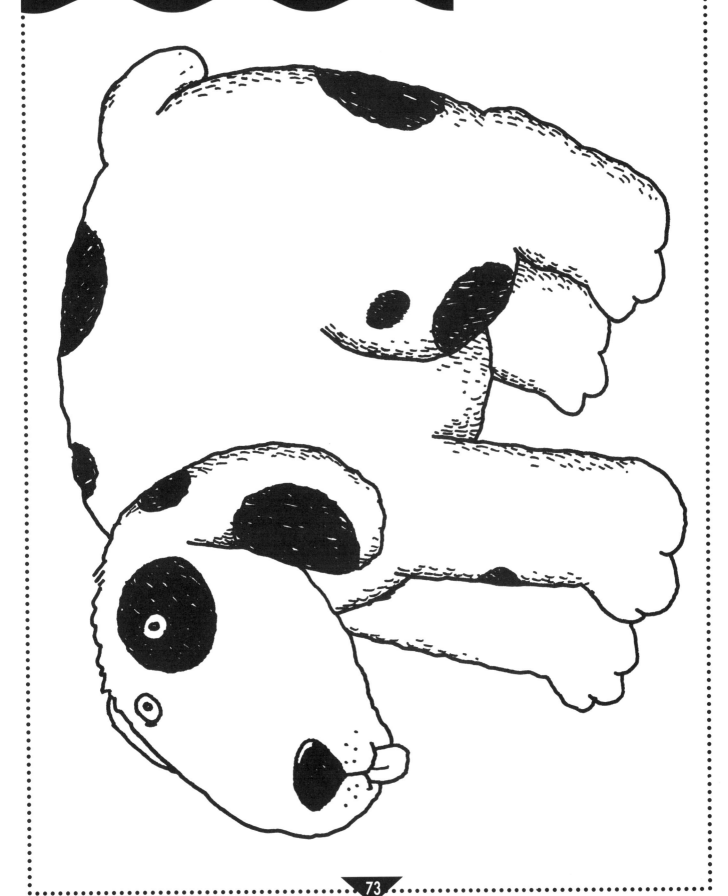

Division Dogs

MATERIALS:

glue
oaktag
scissors
construction paper
single-edged razor blade or artist's knife
tape
cellophane
crayons or markers
paints and paintbrushes

DIRECTIONS:

1. To make the stencils on pages 76–80, reproduce the patterns once. Then mount the stencils on oaktag and cut the shapes out with the razor blade or artist's knife, taking care not to cut into the border area. The stencils may be used in several ways.

2. Trace the stencil onto oaktag several times. Cut out all the patterns. Let students use the stencils to trace the patterns wherever desired.

3. Trace the stencil onto construction paper. Use a razor blade or an artist's knife to cut out the interior of the stencil. Students may tape cellophane over the hole to make a stained-glass interior or use the stencil as a die-cut cover for a greeting card.

4. Students may make collages using one or more of the stencils. Show the children how to overlap tracings of the stencils on a piece of construction paper. Then provide students with crayons or markers or paints to use to color in their collages.

Holiday Stencils

Holiday Stencils

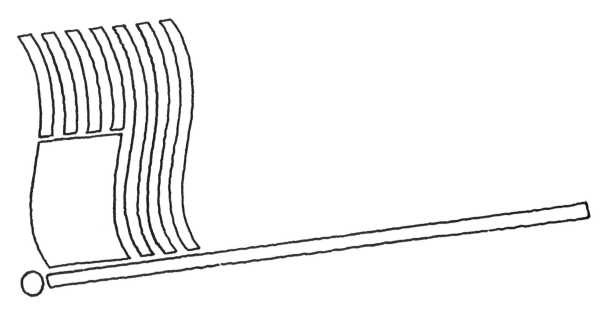

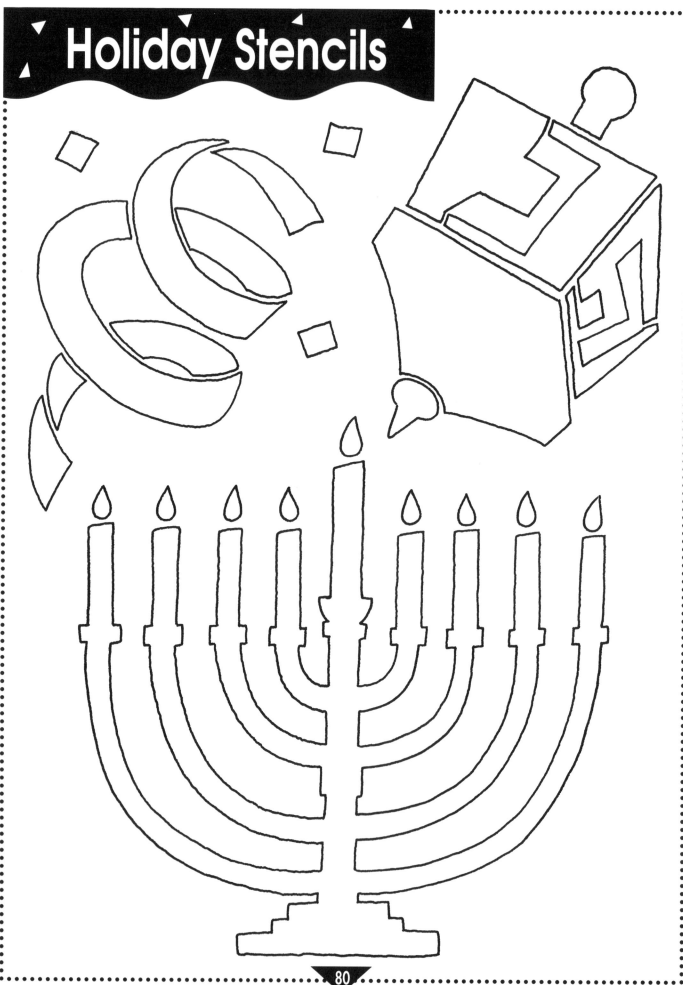

Homemade Paint

Use this recipe to create your own paint to use for classroom decorating.

MATERIALS:

large mixing bowl
wooden spoon
saucepan
7 1/2 cups water
3 cups flour
4 tablespoons salt
3/4 cup sugar
tempera paints
plastic containers

DIRECTIONS:

1. Using a wooden spoon, stir together water, flour, salt, and sugar in a large mixing bowl.
2. Cook in a saucepan over medium heat for approximately 8 to 10 minutes, or until the mixture starts bubbling.
3. Cool, and then place in plastic containers and refrigerate.

4. To make different colors, mix a small amount of the base paint with approximately 1/4 cup of liquid tempera paint. Make red, blue, and yellow paint. Then mix these colors together to make green, purple, orange, and other colors.
5. This paint should be used on thick paper. Students may use paintbrushes and craft sticks to make textured designs with the paints.

All That Glitters

MATERIALS:

aluminum foil
glue
tissue paper
glitter
oaktag (optional)
craft sticks

DIRECTIONS:

1. Give each child a piece of aluminum foil approximately 12" long.
2. Tell students to use craft sticks to cover one side of the aluminum foil with a thin layer of glue.
3. Provide students with tissue paper. Have students rip pieces of the tissue paper and arrange them in a collage on the tacky aluminum foil.
4. Use craft sticks to add another layer of glue over the layer of tissue paper. The tissue paper should become wet from the glue and look paintlike. Have children continue in this manner until each student is satisfied with his or her design.
5. Let students add glitter on top of the last layer of tissue paper.
6. Students may frame their designs by cutting out pieces of oaktag to make a frame and then decorating the frame as they wish. Or they may use the designs to wrap pencil holders, storage boxes, or other containers in the classroom.

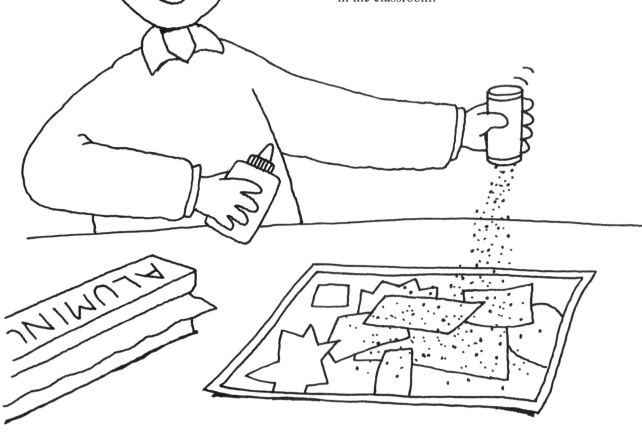

Prehistoric Artists

MATERIALS:

large, flat rocks
dirt, stones, bricks
fruit (strawberries, blueberries, avocado)
vegetable oil
pieces of bark

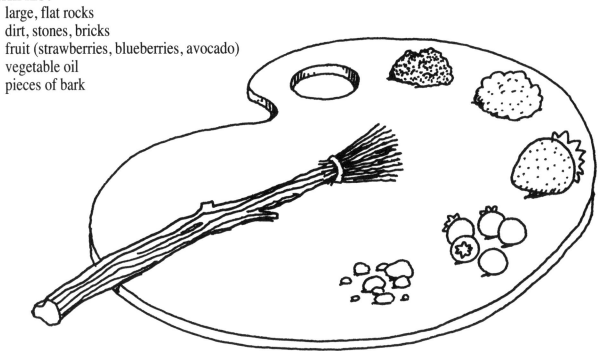

DIRECTIONS:

1. Tell students that they will be creating paintings the way prehistoric people did long ago. Begin by having each student bring in a large, flat rock to use as a painting surface.
2. Help students collect different kinds of dirt or mud, small stones that will crumble easily, and pieces of brick.
3. Have a group of students use larger rocks to crush the stones and brick pieces into powder to make paints.
4. Ask another group of students to mash strawberries, blueberries, avocados, or other fruits to use as paints as well.
5. Mix a small amount of vegetable oil with each powder or fruit to make the paint.
6. Encourage students to use homemade paintbrushes. Students may wish to take a piece of bark and strip away one end to make a brush or simply attach a piece of cotton to a stick with a rubber band.
7. Have students paint designs on their rocks. Display the finished work in the art center or history center under the title "Prehistoric Artists."

Research Race Poster

© 1996 Troll Creative Teacher Ideas

DIRECTIONS:

1. Reproduce the Research Race Poster on pages 85–86 once. Color the poster, mount it on oaktag, and cut it out.

2. Write the names of the children in the class, in alphabetical order, down the left-hand column of the poster.

3. Tell students that they will be playing a game that involves library research. Each week before the class visits the school library, write several questions on the chalkboard that can be answered by visiting a particular area of the library. Begin with 000-90 in the Dewey Decimal System, and progress through the 900s. For example, if the area being covered is the 800s, you may wish to ask a question such as "Name a poem written by T.S. Eliot." Students would then look up T.S. Eliot in the card catalog, locate a book of his poems, and then write down the title of one poem.

4. Be sure to ask several different questions each week so all the children are not researching exactly the same topic.

5. After each student has answered one of the questions correctly, fill in the appropriate box on the Research Race Poster. When each student has all his or her boxes filled in, present him or her with the award on this page.

LIBRARY RESEARCH SKILLS AWARD

PRESENTED TO

_____

_____

_____

Research Race Poster

RESEARCH RACE NAME	000-90	100-190	200-290

Research Race Poster

300-390	400-490	500-590	600-690	700-790	800-890	900-990

The Seven Continents

DIRECTIONS:

1. Reproduce the continents posters on this page and pages 88–92 once. Mount the posters on separate pieces of oaktag and cut them out.

2. Divide the class into seven groups. Assign one continent to each group. Have the groups research the size of the continent, its population, the countries located there, and some of the languages spoken. Ask each group to fill in as much information as they can on the lines provided. Explain that all the information may not always fit and that, on the other hand, they may find more information than they can fit on the poster.

3. Have each group write a short report about each continent. Discuss what makes each continent unique.

4. Attach the posters to a classroom wall or a bulletin board under the title "The Seven Continents."

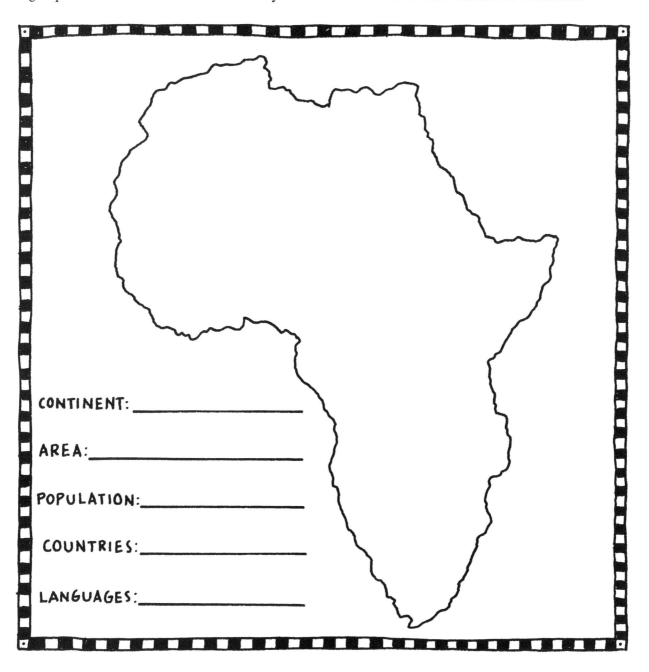

CONTINENT: _____

AREA: _____

POPULATION: _____

COUNTRIES: _____

LANGUAGES: _____

The Seven Continents

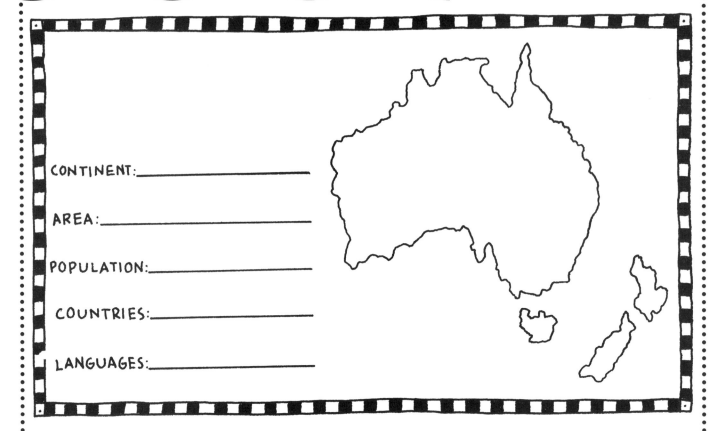

CONTINENT:_____

AREA:_____

POPULATION:_____

COUNTRIES:_____

LANGUAGES:_____

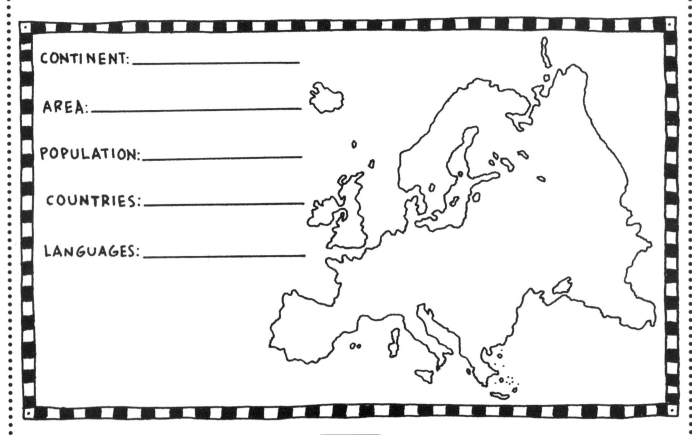

CONTINENT:_____

AREA:_____

POPULATION:_____

COUNTRIES:_____

LANGUAGES:_____

88

The Seven Continents

CONTINENT:_____

AREA:_____

POPULATION:_____

COUNTRIES:_____

LANGUAGES:_____

The Seven Continents

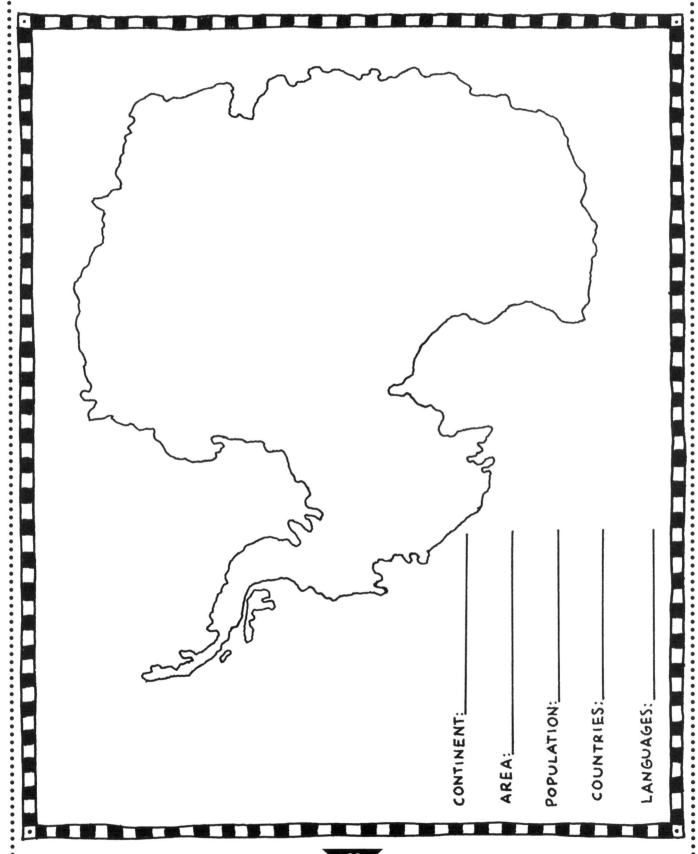

CONTINENT: _____

AREA: _____

POPULATION: _____

COUNTRIES: _____

LANGUAGES: _____

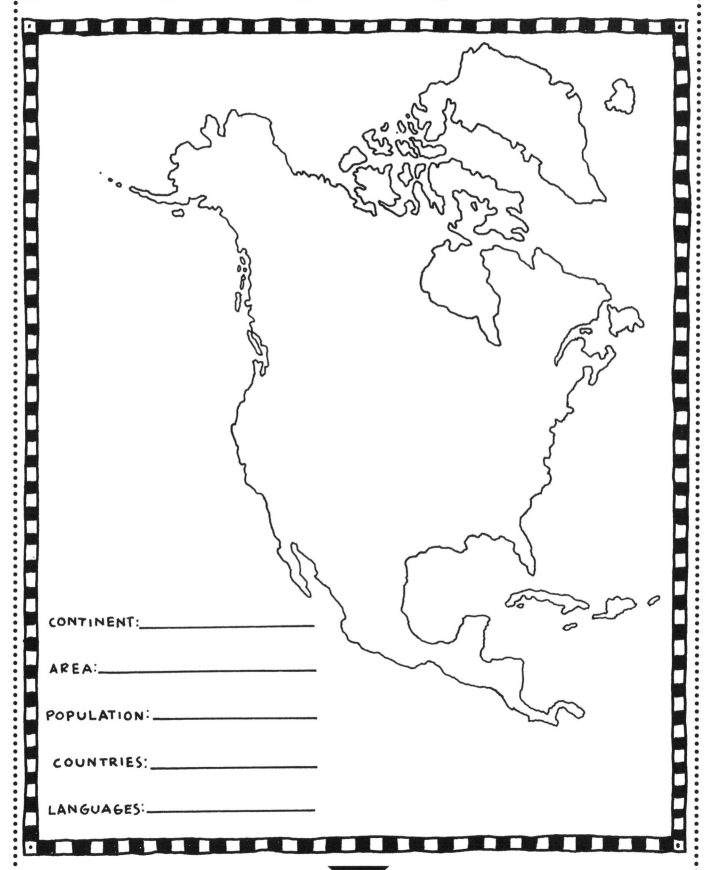

CONTINENT:_____

AREA:_____

POPULATION:_____

COUNTRIES:_____

LANGUAGES:_____

The Seven Continents

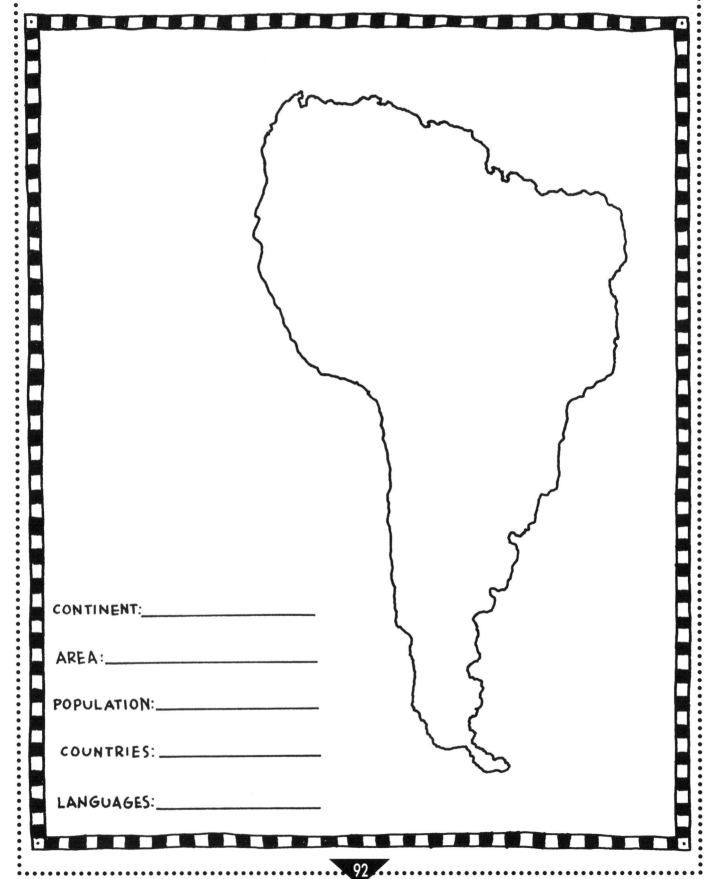

CONTINENT:_____

AREA:_____

POPULATION:_____

COUNTRIES:_____

LANGUAGES:_____

DEAR PARENT,

OUTSTANDING ACHIEVEMENT

IN

Presented to

Presented on _____, 19___ Signed

Awards

1ST

BLUE RIBBON

TO _____

FOR _____

DATE _____

SIGNED _____

CERTIFICATE OF APPRECIATION

TO

FOR

DATE

SIGNED